TRUTH
JASON ABRAMS

I'm the Author and
Just stopped by Northshire
I Hope you enjoy
my book-

10/13/19

Contact: truthpoetrybook@gmail.com

Dedication

To my wife Lauren and my children Jordan & Taylor:

You've inspired me to continue to write the truth. The life we build together is one based on love. Remember to always be kind to one another.

Contents

TRUTH

How you enter, is not how you leave.
Gentle silence fills the mind.
We trust without thought;
Nothing earned.

Doesn't take long to see it fail.
We openly need this path;
Telling all who will listen.
Our trust becomes the friendship.

The faces that light up;
The first moments we walk in.
The innocent peace that doesn't exist;
Painful reality breaks the spirit.

Forged integrity fills the box.
Every face is filled with deceit.
Deception brought with every call;
Tall tales of what it takes to be authentic.

Abandonment creates a new path.
Elated once again.
No longer trapped.
Ready to find new trust.

When we find what makes us whole;
When we trust what makes us happy;
The voice on the other end; earns this respect.
Now we have truth.

CABIN FEVER

The whiskey is poured;
Maybe peace will come his way.
This fearless life he lives haunts
The very breath he takes.

Mornings, filled with laughter;
Evenings are his drifting time—
Higher than the tallest tree,
Lower than the shortest branch.

Dreams are often filled with pain;
Promises are doomed on delivery.
From the snow-covered mountains of the east coast
To the sunny beaches of Southern California.

Here lies the importance of his ability;
He awakens the beast,
Trips across this land,
Wandering from the tips of the clouds.

He rocks in his Kentucky chair,
Sipping cabin fever till the last drop.
Smoothness calms his pain;
The smell will haunt his doubters.

He knows what lies ahead—
The scary nature of reality.
He knows how to handle this—
Pour the syrup.

CANVAS

Our time has come to explode
With empathy.
Stretch my mind through the distinctive
Crossroads of our future.

Breathe air with me that speaks with color,
Flying around my heart like fireflies,
Lighting up the spirit of today,
With defying love for tomorrow.

Here is my captured memory.
Take pride in what I give to you,
Massage the insides to create your own way.

Time is now, breathe with me.
See what my eyes have seen.
Each flowing color pouring out of my tube
Drop by drop onto the canvas.

Creating space with the ink that flows from my fingertips,
The wondrous ways of a simple mind
Has complicated everything in its path,
Destroying the love I have created.

Respecting the taken possibilities,
I have yet to consume you,
Fill you up with my laughter.
Let my fingertips talk to the canvas;
Let me paint you.

FEARED GHOST

Laying there on the side of the road
Wrapped in a blanket to keep me warm,
Strangers pass fearing the unknown,
Bright lights stare me in the face.

I'm here alone, waiting.
I need my way out.
Where's my angel?
The leaves fall as the cold air destroys them.

Lying next to me, she thinks,
Wondering why I can't just get up
And remember all my love.
She thinks she knows what my eyes have seen.

As she travels on without me,
I watch her steps follow a path,
Realizing she's as lost as me...
I'm here alone waiting.

I need my way out.
Where's my angel?
Morning rises and gets me off my feet,
One more day of this will kill me.

I see the light passing by my face,
Walking towards her guides my strength.
The day has proven to be my angel,
Waking up is my way out.

This time I won't let it pass.
I'm awake now for the first time.
I'm here with you,
Not needing a way out.

At peace, I lay here on the ground.
Not waiting, not dying;
Loving and living.

FRIENDSHIP

I have searched for years,
Always coming up empty.
Every soul I pour mine into
Provides emptiness.

What I've been through
Needs to be talked about.
I found myself empty,
Forgotten about my depth.

My true partner in life opened my eyes.
Someone who never crossed my path,
Is the one I needed to hear.
Trust in her, led me to you.

I have opened my demons,
I have expressed my strengths,
Pouring out my limitations
Without fear of an empty feeling.

I've found a true friend in you.
Not always about issues,
Not always about happiness,
Yet my soul has become stronger.

You have opened my mind,
Not just while sitting in the chair.
Through our temple,
Learning the way of life.

I've always been true to me,
Now growing into an even better me.
Taking great pride in our friendship;
I take great strength in your teachings.

GLASS HAND

Trapped within my mind,
Fire screaming from my body,
Intense pressure building,
Wanting to explode into the woods.

My mind needs to expand,
Breathing, bleeding, burning.
My life becomes a volcano,
1,000 years in the making.

All I hear is anger;
All I hear is fear.
I'm the one with the problem.
I cause everything.

My young creative minds are fearful.
Looking up to me is what I've always wanted.
I must not conceal this behavior,
Hiding will only grow the beast.

Change is inevitable in this circle,
Positive or Negative.
She is the fire that molds me;
I hold the outcome in my glass hand.

FIGHTER

Survival of the finest heart,
Forcing nature to the core.
Through the trees I see you,
Creating love through pain.

Passion makes you Follow
A path of strength.
Encouraged by family,
Running through life.

Love is not shown or heard,
Not tasted or smelled,
Not deserved or owed.
Love is earned.

You have earned the love of us all.
You are the reason we try,
We fight,
We live.

I love with strength, I
Cry with pain.
My luck is knowing you,
My love is being you.

I've learned about heart through your friendship,
I've led my life with your strength.
I hold you close to my heart,
You are my brother for life.

My world will always know you,
Always have a presence.
I will teach your strength,
I feel lucky to call you my brother.

My brother for life.

ONE MORE REP

Eyes wide at 4:00 am,
Soft silence with each step.
Around the banister towards the door,
Don't forget the energy bar.

Darkness fills the streets,
Red and green lights ahead.
Around the corner,
Down the dark alley.

Friendly faces gather on the rubber floor,
Foam roller conversations.
A few push-ups,
A few pull-ups.

Coaches bring us in,
Huddled around for an overview of the pain to come.
Few modifications and laughter,
Now we're ready.

Focused faces fill the floor,
Fist bumps and high fives.
This is what we come for,
This is how we start our day.

15 minutes go by,
We lay on the sweaty floor.
Strange smiles fill our faces,
That's our reward.

This place creates strengths of all kinds,
We enter this wanting something more.
We're driven to achieve,
The trust in our coaches is how we get there.

The friendships we create are our foundation,
We pick each other up,
We push each other to keep moving,
The next challenge becomes our focus.

One more rep…

FALLEN STRANGER

Don't hold me back,
I'm looking for a way out.
Don't force my hand,
I need to tell you the truth.

I keep these secrets,
I find these ways,
Down passages,
Through dark streets.

You only see what I provide;
Your vision is what I allow.
I want to release the power,
Force love into the world.

I am here to awaken
The demons that sit beside you.
No longer will I stay silent,
No longer will you have me.

Fear the unknown,
Stretch across the reflection.
Don't sit tight,
You may fall deep.

FEARLESS

Do you feel?
Can you smell the fear,
Bleeding down my face,
Dropping to the ground?

Scratching away
At the deepest sea.
Sharpened teeth
Coral around my heart.

I can see the truth
All around me, deep in the ancient world,
Surrounding my heart,
Dying with my soul.

Breathing alone,
Take me with you.
I am fearless;
I am free to you.

Drowning in this water,
Cold at my feet.
Ripples pass my eyes,
Don't leave me here.

To die without you,
Alone at last.
This is what we need,
A future that has no present.

Can you feel the weight?
Can you see the maze?
Come get lost with me.
You will finally see.

What it means to love
and lose control.
Find a way,
We can be together.

In the mind, the soul,
Every action that takes my innocence.
Don't scratch the surface,
Dig deep and love what you find.

NO ROOM TO HIDE

Each moment I reach out to ask why,
I find nothing in my body to make me scream,
Forcing the outer love,
Bleeding my truth to an unknown heart.

She won't bleed her storm,
It breathes down her back.
Not to unfold upon her warmth and to
Extend my youthfulness.

Preach to the world that I am not common.
I can be taught,
I can be truthful,
I can love.

But I will not give up;
I will fight to the death.
Of my crazy red blood,
Some need to make it painful.

Stretch it, force me down Inside
The mountain of glory.
You Will rise upon this respect;
You Will be given my future.

Toy with my emotions,
And you will find nothing.
An empty hole,
Where my heart once thumped.

Pouring out massive amounts of trust,
Throwing it back into the wild thorns.
Rose petals fallen to the ground,
Leaving impressions which have no explanation.

Here is where I confuse the wondering eyes;
Here lies my faith,
Protecting each step with caution.
Here lies me.

Don't pretend to not be yourself.
You are seen through a window
That is as dark as you are.
Don't hide.

You will be caught...

EARN EVERY STEP

I sit here and think what to write.
Ideas created by mindless opportunities,
Stressful moments running through my head,
I need to feel that pressure build up.

With every leaf that falls to the ground,
Dying with beautiful color on its way down.
Every rain drop that falls from the sky,
Hitting her face forming tears.

Why does her heart bleed with water?
Her cherished moments disappear in the wind.
I want her to feel what I feel;
The loss of such love brings great questions.

Why I am here?
Why do I go through this?
What can I learn?
Will I feel this?

It's time for me become a man,
Earn every step that I take,
Force the wonderful emotion,
Love, live and beyond…

SHOES UNTIED

Crossing the world with my shoes untied,
Living everyday as a beautiful lie.
Sitting here wondering can I dream a different dream,
Or will he have his way and go to extremes?

With every check that I earn,
 I don't get 2 steps,
And my laces are caught in the trap.

Time to wake up,
Not be afraid of losing.
I'll always have her by my side,
So I'm never alone.

Who knew changing the station would be this hard.
I've been listening to this song my whole life,
Always waiting to write my own,
Loving that I now get the chance.

I will change my ways,
Grab life by the bolts,
And put them together on my own.
I've even got a plan.

My day starts today,
With my shoes laced up.

CROSSING PATHS

Where do I go from this path?
Jumping over the cracks in the road,
Trying not to break her back,
But always seeming to do so.

I love her because of what she's done for me,
Always trying to gain more respect for her.
But not from me,
In my hidden way, I push another.

But he won't budge.
His eyes wonder the sky as we drive down the road,
I try to keep him focused,
Fail every time.

I keep quiet about my details.
Not my right to interject,
But that causes me to lie.
I'm at the edge sometimes, and I burst.

The more silent I am, the angrier I get,
The more I get in trouble.
My silence is my enemy,
An enemy who always seems to win.

She doesn't understand my ways,
My frustration.
She's accepted a certain life
And lashes out at me.

Maybe her frustration angers her,
To take his side, because that's her choice?
Why make it more difficult for her life?

Why make those paths cross?

Will we never see the same path?
There's no need.
Having a different heart is growth,
Different as always scares the ones we love.

The teacher is usually afraid of the unknown.
The student takes his chance on the wild card.
Achieve growth through my eyes,
Get there on my back.

The man I am becoming
Pleases me and is someone I love.
That's what makes it all worth it,
The love of her heart.

DEPARTURE

Through fierce emotions
I travel above the line,
Seeking love for myself
And passion for my future.

Worry not what he has done;
Worry not what he will do.
My promise now
Is engraved in my foot print.

The trail I leave behind;
My beautiful hair,
My soft touch.
Watch as I walk away.

My lips are genuine
And sealed for love.
Pretending to be yours no longer,
The taste you will never have.

Woman as I am,
In this moment of pure intensity,
My body filled with excitement,
Racing through my blood.

I have become me.
The soul that protects my heart.
One that is not yours to touch;
Is mine to love.

DESIRE

At times we feel a loss
Common to our hearts,
Falling to the ground,
As a drifting snowflake.

Searching for the true moment,
Feeling emptiness,
Accompanied by truth,
Distraught by nature.

This is the love that I have.
Creations abruptly stopped,
Failure throughout the colony,
Pressure arrives by loss.

We hold this moment,
Impatiently lusting over our desire,
Arriving in unknown forces.
She has appeared in my heart.

Shadowing my fears,
Standing tall next to me,
Never forgetting why she's there,
Never losing her passion.

Creating this space,
We occupy with strength.
Awaiting beauty,
With desire to love.

HEAR ME

It's time for me to open my eyes,
She's there for me to love.
Walking through the trees,
Stepping on the branches,

Cracking souls through the air.
I see her smile cutting the sky,
Scaring me to the end of the earth,
Find me this cushion.

Stretch across my heart,
Feel as I do, on the day it starts
To heal and burn.
It's there I start to learn.

Finding my way to the point of destruction.
Even-though we're creating space,
I can never can get away.
Space only allows time to think.

Think, the moment of all truths,
Here and now the distinct point of view.
My timeline to this happiness,
That involves every drop of blood.

Tasting the moments that I need,
Pushing forward without action.
Wet drops of salt make a puddle below my feet.
That's when I see myself,
My true self.

MOMENT

See the world
in reflection,
I can hear her voice
making music.

Simple words loving me,
I am here just to be.
Here is me and now is my will,
The time I know is standing still.

Just one moment, and I'll be back,
Holding closely this heart-attack.
One more time creating space,
Wish you could see my face.

Clouds of glory, create this moment.
Trust in the fruit gone forever.
So I do trust in you, one more day,
One more you.

REACHING

The moments chosen,
Scared to the touch.
Incredible strength,
Way too much.

Truth has begun
Despite the fear.
Screaming fights,
Hear the despair.

Take away this fear,
Hear the desire.
Right in front of you,
Sits crystal fire.

Amaze my intention,
Watch my glory.
Tear apart,
Hear my story.

I sit here now,
Writing into you.
Drops of salt,
Leave no clue.

TOUCH

Don't be alarmed,
He sits with you.
Strong minded,
Free willed.

Don't be afraid,
She waits for you.
Happy eyes,
Lifted Spirit.

I hear you speak,
Lovely in my mind.
Gentle forces,
Reaching out.

Time is near, Scared
to the touch.
Incubus is upon you,
Don't close your eyes.

Feel the touch,
Lose your mind.
To the edge,
Release your body.

Lay back,
Love what you are.
Force nothing,
Embrace the soul.

YOU REMAIN

Can't sleep tonight,
I miss your touch.
I want to dream with you,
Feel your warmth inside.

Sitting beneath the stars,
I crack a smile.
Wishing you were next to me,
Just for a while.

Cross the street,
Sit down with strangers.
It's here and now.
I can feel the danger.

Who will you be?
Surrounding my love,
Distance carrying my soul,
Bring me back to calm.

Your warm words
Fill me up.
Strength inside me
Lifts my passion.

Here is my time,
I won't have to wait.
You will arrive
On your own.

Hold me up,
Shine through the stars,
The moon fades away,
Yet you remain.

SALT WATER

Walk with me,
Stare up at the ghosts
That form from our ocean,
Blanketing my mind.

Take my hand,
The truth is beside you,
Reacting to the unknown,
Feeling me inside.

Puddles of reflection,
Creating images of our soul.
Tiny crystal movements,
Shadowing my steps.

Subtle lips,
Attacking my heart.
Strength is shown;
Restraint is needed.

HULK

In search of who I am,
Digging deep within my soul.
Can't seem to find my direction,
A traveler at best.

Intense stress with his presence,
Freedom without it.
Why can't I let go?
How hard should this be?

Years of frustration,
Leading to empty moments.
My life has everything,
Yet I can't control it.

Is my past altering my present?
That of who I can't control has
Found its way into my life,
Searching in the wrong places.

Does all of the bad live within me?
A fault does not appear,
Yet truths are my reality.
Control is lost.

I must find a way to harness,
The past will not reveal through me,

I value what we've created.
I must overcome these issues.

Am I hiding behind a mask?
These issues are mine to own.
They should live with me;
They should be dealt with by me.

The Angry Hulk appears at the worst times.
Is there ever a good time?
This must be contained.
I have to learn to control the beast.

My family depends on my control.
I depend on my happiness;
I will change this behavior.
Fear disappears.

TINY STEPS

Tiny steps down the hallway,
Fearless smiles ear to ear,
Laughter filled with love,
Moments that never fade.

Words only begin to tell a story,
Through her innocent eyes.
Every step is brand new;
Every fall hurts for the first time.

We can protect her,
We can help her,
We can love her,
But we can't hide her.

She will learn with Pain,
She will love with Joy,
Every day is brand new;
Every moment is amazement.

She is our heart,
She is our love,
She is our best,
She is…our daughter.

BEING A FATHER

I will go to the end of the earth,
Travel at any time of day or night,
Run until my feet hurt,
Climb until I'm out of breath.

Hug as long as I want,
Hold her when she cries,
Laugh with her when she's happy,
Make her food when she's hungry.

Pick her up when she falls,
Comfort her at 3 am when she needs me,
Rack up sleepless nights;
Smile and stay awhile.

Run home to the adventure,
Just so she knows I'm there.
Put my life on hold to make her smile,
Which makes me smile.

Some people don't understand,
Need to judge,
They say these ways are confusing.
Pretending to show interest.

All she knows is her Father loves her,
I've earned this right,
I've waited my whole life to have a family,
Nothing can stop my heart.

A father's love is shown
Through a daughter's smile.
This is the father I love to be.

SHADOWED SOUL

Tears fall from a man's face,
Proud of what he sees.
The vision of helping a cause,
Dreaming of the unknown.

Feeling pressure above his eyes,
Awakening the sleeping giant,
Surrounding his heart,
Loving his soul.

Scared each time the moment drops,
Into a puddle of illusion.
Screaming above the tree tops,
Falling through the ice.

A moment is felt through his heart,
Realizing his freedom is in jeopardy.
The desire for love is his only secret,
Now the road has changed.

The one who showed him love,
Keeps his heart close,
Following her steps through sweat,
Keeping her name within reach.

The shadows become his getaway,
His pain becomes their existence,
Searching for one who loves as she does,
Not reachable in his life.

He loves the woman who values family,
Who understands real snow,
Who realizes what makes him tick,
Who he knows loves him back.

RED COAT

Stretch across the table,
Read above the lines.
Here and now you may find me appealing,
This little wing with brightness of colors.

Flocking to the soul,
I hear her heart thumping down the road.
Pebbles and dirt fly into my face,
Touch me.

Wipe away these fears,
What you cannot feel
Is that of my lust,
Breathing down the neck of the next soul.

My eyes open with tenderness,
Always blurry through the leaves.
Her Hot Red coat glares within me,
Forcing blood out through my eyes.

I want her to feel this intensity,
Screaming to get out of my body.
I want to kiss her lips;
I want to hold her close.

I want to love her.

SLEEP WELL

Standing tall and proud,
She waits by the window.
Her eyes see wings,
Reaching to touch.

Subtle hints of green
Soar through the air.
Moments moving
Inside her body.

Lust creating emotion,
Pouring out of her mouth,
Like a red wine waterfall
Never reaching the ground.

This gentle silk
Draped across her body.
Glowing from her heart,
Awakens my body.

Her desire is blind,
Feeling her way
Through my impulse,
Scratching at the glass.

Gentle kisses awaken her body,
Feeling her clutch the sheets as
My lips control her,
And put her to sleep.

PATIENT

My eyes wide open,
Staring with envy.
Not to close,
Tears will shed.

Touch of her hair,
Soft against my face.
Feeling excited,
For moments wasted.

Don't tell the world,
Secrets lay in the heart.
Calm setting,
Within her body.

Drops of red,
Filling the glass.
An evening of subtlety,
Created warmth in the air.

A night that should be
Tender.
Was all that it should be.
Patient.

KISS

Soft to the touch,
Yearning for a reason,
Wanting passion,
Pressed up against your heart.

Feeling the truth,
Tasting the force,
Covered by uniqueness,
Layered with love.

Lips pressed together,
Eyes lock in place.
Warmth takes over your body,
You touch them gently.

Then share a kiss so wonderful,
Your body drops with emotion.
And I am there to catch you and
Kiss you again...

CAN YOU HEAR ME?

I wonder if you can hear me,
I know you're way up high.
But I think you should listen,
I never seem to lie.

I see you running, up and down the streets.
I wonder if you'll ever want to sit with me.
And just pretend that nothing's ever wrong.
And live a life with me as I tell you through this song.

Your simple actions never mean to hurt.
But the pain they cause drops me to the dirt.
You're out there conquering and finding purpose.
 I hope what you seek takes you very far.

And when I see you, sometime in the distance,
I hope you remember me and maybe then you'll listen.
To the many dreams I've had, together running free.
In them you stay with me, on the same side of the street.

I realize it's over, but I'll always wonder why.
You came through me and stunned my life.
So I sit here without you and miss you just the same.
And I know it's best for us, to wonder a different frame.

I wonder if that day will come, when we share the heart again.
And start our life together and continue this run.
It's the simple things in life that bring me to my knees.
I wonder if it's really you who understands me.

Listen closely, I'm driving down this road.
I admit a bit lonely, but I like to be alone.
Maybe she's lonely too, no shoes on her feet.
I think she's the one who will finally understand me.

STRUGGLE WITH ME

Struggle with me,
I know it's only once.
But I see the door is opening,
And so easily I can fall.

To my knees
To ask you that question.
Will you stay with me,
And lift me off this street?

I know you're alone sometimes,
I see you sitting there.
I'm scared to ask you,
I'm scared to stare.

See these little things of mine,
I want to set them free.
Each time I breathe,
You can understand me.

Yes those are my wishes,
I know they seem simple.
What I want in life,
Simply put, is you.

Ready for terror.
I think it's time for war.
Do you see in the distance?
Yes, I know it's far.

But come closer,
You're standing in the dark.
Hard to see your face,

Shinning through this spark.

Can you see us now,
Or do you just see dust?
My tracks are deep, I know,
I struggle with the lust.

TINY CRYSTALS OF SAND

Time runs by us like a shooting star,
Flashes of moments soaring by our eyes.
Remember the times of deception,
Times of promise.

It's what we create for the future
That makes us keep going.
We try to change what has happened,
Can't be done.

Moving forward is the only way,
To understand the ways of our heart.
Challenges that come with our uncertainty,
Little crystals of happy moments.

All difficult times, yet we push through them.
For there will be moments we need to remember,
And hopefully we won't want to change what happened.
There are beautiful steps for us.

They make my world happy when I entertain
The thought of our future.
Tough times, easy times,
I want them all with you.

PRECIOUS TIMES

These precious times
Travel through our hearts,
Seeming to strike fear along the way.
The simple one speaks highly of you.

Strangely in and out of your life,
But never out of your heart.
He strives, he continues,
He needs to know your desires.

When will it come to him?
How far can he run?
This is the time to awaken,
This life that's in front of you.

Every step that is taken,
Breathes alone in reality.
Together in spirit,
They shall see each other's faces.

Now, only in our dreams.
When will they become one?
Time goes by without a blink,
Love always seeming to travel with them.

Joined together from earlier days,
Her beauty holds a place in his heart.
There's room for her to fit,
The time is now, but for now, I sit.

GENTLE BEAUTY

Slowly, she walks in from my past,
Cold, fresh air on the tip of her nose,
Bundled up, clinging to her body,
Desperately creating warmth.

Her head rises slowly,
A gentle smile appears that lights up the room.
A feeling overcomes me,
Creating a smile of my own.

As we enter the room,
Flashes of light sparkle in her eyes.
A touch of her hair as I pass by;
Glimpse at her walk.

As I sit on the white suede,
My head turns towards her.
We lock eyes, and my world may begin to change,
The girl I knew so young becomes a woman.

A surprise of passion,
Excites me, intrigues me.
My memory captures my soul.
Not to leap, yet patience has become me.

She shines in a new light,
An unexpected ray.
Those times can be tender,
Beautifully surprised.

AWAITING THE MOMENT

Awaiting the moment,
Patiently wanting to hold her.
Deep breaths of the ocean floor,
Find their way to my soul.

Protect me from the uncertainty,
Roll with me down this path.
Reaching out to touch her as she passes by,
Catching only the ghost.

I need this passion that fills my heart
To unravel towards her soul,
Cushioning the fall from the clouds,
Passing by cold air.

Determination I do not need.

CEDE

I surrender the power I do not have,
Creation of a mind that figures on its own;
Beautiful butterflies stretching across the sky,
Creating a blanket that covers my heart.

I surrender to the woman;
She knows best of what we think we know.
I speak to be outspoken,
I reach to be outreached.

My love has no limits,
Yet they are found through your mind.
What I see inside is not real,
You tell me what is real.

The touch of your skin,
The flow of your hair.
Softness of our lips coming together,
Your blood starts to rise.

Overtaken throughout your body,
Passion consumes you.
Aggressiveness is upon me,
The moment has arrived.

I surrender.

FROM THE INSIDE

Every time I see her face
It wakens me to a different place.
Strange times find me,
They seek me out.

And my time is here,
And my time is near,
To the moment of expression,
I can feel your power.

I can feel your destiny,
It breathes by my side,
Travels through my heart,
And out the other...world of deception.

It comes and comes loud;
It brings, and it brings me soul,
To think of me as a whore,
In this the world.

A free spirt to the mountains;
The more I look the more I take.
It grabs me by the moments that touch my insides,
Feels deeper than I've traveled so far.

It's here, on the inside,
And it speaks to the one who sees,
The only person who believes
And sits next to me, dying in my arms.

NEW WAYS

I can relate to you every day of my life,
But I can't think of anything else to say.
I can dream of you tonight,
But I don't want to let loose on my life.

I try, but I can't see the future.
So tempting and out of reach you say,
Once to me, I drove you away,
And captured my heart in many ways.

I've fallen, I've cried,
Hitting the bottom of the sea,
Rubbing against her, reaching out;
Love me, want me, I need you inside.

This time is precious;
You're waiting, and now we can be one.
Take my hand, stretch it out;
It's our time to be loved.

I'M HERE ALONE

It's a pitch-black night when I hit the road;
My eyes are tired and laying low.
As I drive by open lanes,
I tap my ear to hear a little better,
On the other end he's there to drive me home.

I pass another big rig to my right,
The new black road's in my sight,
And the smell of the tar creeps in through the window,
He's there so often, I can't remember him not being there.

I'm here alone,
I'm here to trust myself,
I'm here to welcome her to my life,
I'm here alone,
But not for long.

Just as soon as I grow up,
We'll be alone.
She puts the drink on my table,
And asks me if I need anything else.
Thank you, ma'am, I'm doing fine,
Just leave me to rest.

I wake up, and I lose an hour,
Off the plane headed to Texas.
As I pick my head up,
I see her smile.
She's open arms, she's been ready for a while.

No longer alone;
I can trust her too.
She welcomes me as I welcome her;
No longer alone.
We're together for now,
I've finally grown up,
We're not alone.

MY LOVE

Tiny moments from my past,
They stand tall in my face,
Making sure I don't forget
What an impact she had on me.

Lessons I learned from her first moment of love,
Sweet apple samples left behind on my windshield,
Always letting me know,
She loves me.

Cherished moments of our past helped us get to where we are,
True ideas of what love really was at that moment.
For what it was then, we loved,
And for what it is now, we love.

Our lives have moved forward without each other,
But always by her side if she should ever need me again.
Some paths never get uncrossed,
And that's what makes it worth it.

The true people in our lives,
They touch us in certain ways that can't be understood.
Just to be there and show unconditional passion,
Is what my life has been about,

And what I continue to strive for.
I've always known where I stand,
And she's always known that my heart will never leave her side;
Although my heart is different,
She will have it forever in a way
Only she can understand.

I feel lucky to have certain people in my life,
Years pass by us so quickly.
I like to think no matter how many do pass,
Our lives will always cross in our hearts.

BEAUTIFUL LOVE

I know her face,
I see her across the room when my eyes meet the sun.
She's precious in the way she moves,
Her walk, tender.

The way she makes her coffee,
Just enough not spill over the edge.
The way she breaks her eggs and leaves half in the shell,
A gentle smile as she stirs.

The warmth of her heart brings a smile to my face.
I love her unique ways.
Striking as she walks down the stairs,
Even as we fill our hunger with burgers from the dive down the street.

It's not where we are, it's that we're together.
Such a wonderful feeling comes over me when I think of her,
See her, touch her,
Just to be around her.

Amazing that some people don't see that in their partner.
I'd like to know what drove them the other way.
The most delicate of issues;
The hardest of times.

Let's be the cute, old couple on the bench at the park;
They sit and feed the birds,
Holding each other as if
There's no-one else there.

That's beautiful love.

MISSING YOU

When you think of someone,
What do you see in them?
When you see them walking towards you,
What do you think of?

Do you just see how beautiful they are?
Do you think to yourself how they make you feel?
Is it about you?
Is it about them?

When I think of you,
I see strength.
I see a woman who takes charge,
but also knows how to love and step back.

When I think of you,
I see a woman I want to be around.
Not for myself,
But for the pure fact that it's wonderful to be around you.

Observing the things that drive you,
Watching you pull in the sails,
Kick a soccer ball,
Run a race.

Just watching you be you,
Can make someone love you.
Wanting to be near you means
More than just that.

It means love...and there is love there somewhere.

It hides well, but more and more it's coming out...

CATCH AND RELEASE

I'm trapped, I feel unlucky.
I walk through the door every day waiting to walk out.
It's the first thing on my mind,
the last thing I know how to do.

I have the whole world in front of me,
At this ripe young age.
Yet I can't seem to break free,
Chains are too tight.

I want to feel the passion
that drives my soul.
This is what I want to,
but I can't let go.

I try to learn from his mind,
He's been through so much.
Somehow he can't release me,
because of everything he's missed.

Rough patches create space,
I'll pick myself up with you at my side.
As I sit here every day,
I wonder what could be.

The longer I wait, the further away the dream gets,
But it does remain to be my driving force.
Nothing will get in my way of smiling with my real love.

BLINDED DREAM

Why can't the life I want be the life I lead?
What makes us so vulnerable to the poisons of life?
It's time to make a change and not be scared;
I've let go of something wonderful.

Maybe it's to find something amazing.
I've opened the door for anyone to come and go as the please,
But lately, once they enter I make them leave before I know their name,
Letting go is something we're not prepared to do.

Human nature tells us not to let go, but to keep them close in our hearts.
It's the phrase let go that gets us.
We can let go and still love,
We can cherish the times we had and prepare for a new heart.

I wonder if I can do that;
Am I strong enough to find amazing?
Do I even know what that takes?
Or am I too blind to know that I see it every day in my dreams?

Yet I can't grasp her heart,
It's difficult because it's special.
It's beautiful because she's calm.

The time to unwrap is now.

I think it's time we find out...

BROKEN HEART, HEALED

A new breakthrough in his heart.
He has no idea what will hit him,
Even if he reacts with comfort,
He'll still have lost the desire.

How can it come to this?
What can go so wrong in love that it gets to this point?
Aren't we supposed to know before we get into it?
Immaturity in a place that it can't exist.

I say it shows me nothing, and leaves a bad example,
When in reality it shows me what not to do,
Needing to take the right steps towards my own family,
Making sure that love is my direction not a certain mold.

Making it last 50 years lying in bed next to a ghost,
That can't be explained,
Something you don't look for.
Love is a part of us and will hit us at the right moments.

Hopefully we're smart enough to grab hold.

FAMILY GEM

In the darkness of the sky,
Out shines a beauty.
A soul recognized by her strength
And courage.

She amazes
She overcomes,
Always looking ahead to the next difficult trip.

She left the nest years ago,
Yet you can always feel her love around the family.
We can turn to her at any time,
Never worrying about denial.

A true Friend, Daughter, and Sister.

Out of her heart pours a caring thought,
Showing me that love can come from
Outside the family with such sincerity,
Making me trust what love really means.

And the love of friends and family,
A critical part of my future in this world.

WAKE UP AND SMILE

Wake up and smile.
Can't hide from the sun.
Pleasantries shared from the barrel of the gun,
Now you're sleeping for good.

Nightmares appear every time you close your eyes,
Struggling with the thought that makes you cry.
Your vision's not shared,
No-one sees your mind.

You can't help but run and hide,
All the time.
You feel alone and sad,
Weak and mad.

All of this time,
We were here for you,
Just pick up the phone.
I'll be here on the other end.

Wake up and smile.
It's amazing he can be so shallow,
And then watch it all float away.
I'm confused.

With my whole life.
But who in this world
Isn't like that?
I am the ghost?

Aren't we all a little lost?
I can think of crazy imaginations.
I think of the way we should be,

I think of when we die.

Am I wasting your time?
Do I push too much ?
Or maybe not enough,
Will you let me know?

Or die alone?

SUBTLENESS

I'm falling into place.
Comfortable conversation.
Troubled times shared,
Finding out her secrets,
Her desires.

We are forced to discover the unknown.
Many go through this time and never learn,
Blind to the many possibilities of why it will fail.
Never hearing a reason why,
Never took the time to figure it out.

Different takes on a new meaning.
True experiences that create so much interest,
Is it our unknown that attracts us to each other?
Or true attraction?

This unique situation intrigues me.
Her ways are beautiful and tough.
Never have I spoken about a woman's beauty,
Without talking about the way she looks,
Until now.

Cracking her shell is not what it's about,
Staying the way we are is.

Not changing the subtle ways that first attracted me,
We remain us and interlock the new creations.
What will we find in the end
Remains to be seen.

TRAVELING MIND

My mind travels every which way,

Before hitting a wall.
It's tender, and I push as hard as I can,
Never reaching the point of success.

I want to be at peace with myself.
I want to travel the thoughts of its beauty.
Understanding the power, it has,

And yearning for a weakness so

I just can't seem to find what I'm looking for.
Maybe I need to stop thinking of me,

And find out what makes her happy.

Maybe then and only then, Will I become a man.

One who gives and does not need to receive, In time will
have everything he wants.
Love...

SPECIAL CONFUSION

There are so many challenges in our lives.
Colors that fade too quickly,
And roads that end without a sign.

What carries me through each day,
Is knowing that others are out there,
Others that touch us in a unique way.

You don't fall in love with every soul you meet,
But there are some out there that have something special.
Just to know them is to be rewarded.

We come across people every day, and you know,
When it's something different, you know.
Something real, something Beautiful.

We like to challenge ourselves repeatedly,
To make sure we know where we are.
May lose ourselves along the way,
But at least we started the walk.

We could even lose her along the way,
An even greater loss,
An even greater hill to climb.

Just knowing someone that can touch you that much,
How they can get inside your soul
And reach down, grabbing every inch on the way through.

Either tearing it apart or healing the wound.
It can overwhelm you to the point of confusion,
But something about her moves us.

We need to figure out what it is.
Could come up empty handed, but at least the moment
I could share with her.

Moments like that create something.
Finding out what that something is
Can be exciting and disappointing.

RISKS

I piqued her interest.
She smiles with innocence,
But I cannot see.

Taking risks like that can have fatal results.
What's failure without trying?
It gives no meaning to love.

Devotion must be introduced and taken seriously.
A world without it is a world I'll never know.
I strive to learn those who touch me,

When I come across a new heart,
Such as the one I touched, I know the effort must be put forward

You can't lose what you never had.

LETTING GO

As I sit here in darkness,
Watching the shadows on the wall,
It is her that I see,
In this bed where I fall.

I'm covered in theory,
From my head to my toe.
She's a huge piece of me,
But I must let her go.

I wonder where I'll be,
When years pass us by,
Waiting for love,
With the absence of my life.

Or will she wake up one day,
Next to me and say,
"I loved you from the start;
Here's where I'll stay."

Protect her in this moment,
Until we are free.
We will always have us,
But this is how it shall be.

ANGRY YOUNG MAN

I'm an angry young man.
Help me with this project,
Don't push me down,
Don't bury my needs.

I'm not who you are,
I can't be what you want me to be,
The depth is too great,
The mountain is too high.

I am who I am,
Love me for me,
Stay by my side,
Stand tall with me.

Love me for what I can give,
Care for me for what I can do,
Support my choices,
Be proud of what I will do.

YOUNG ANGER

Happy, innocent boy waiting to learn,
Four years old.
A child unaware,
Scared and empty.

I'm angry and hurt,
I'm missing the love I deserve,
I'm missing the comfort I desire,
Learning how to hate.

Feeling alone.
Time to wake up and comfort,
Make sure she's taken care of,
We're just kids, but we need each other.

Yearning for patience.
What I need now is simple.
Now is the time to show it,
The support I need is easy.

I know enough at four to know it gets
worse. Be there for us,
Do what you're supposed to do,
Take care of us now.

MY SILENT VOICE

I can hear your voice,
Can feel your hug,

See your smile,
Smell your sweetness.

Struggling to tell you with my voice,
Only means the effort is there.
These small moments of pain
Are real because I try so hard.

You are my rock;
Everything we do together makes me stronger.
Laughing is my greatest pleasure, and in that moment,
I feel everyone around me.

Feeling trapped is a real emotion,
Allowing me to feel that
Helps me overcome my physical limits;
It's ok that I go through this.

I am strong because you teach me to be;
I cry because you show me it's ok to feel.
With my weakest moments,
Come my greatest strengths.

How we choose to define ourselves,
Will continue to control the outcome.
My reality is guided by our family;
Nothing can stop us.

WHY

Why am I always afraid?
Every day I want to cry.
My life is perfect,
I have everything I've ever wanted.

Beautiful wife,
Two beautiful, innocent daughters;
Smiles are endless in our family,
Love surrounds our home.

My wife is strong,
My wife is smart,
She's an amazing mother;
My kids are loved unconditionally.

My family, present in both directions,
The support is endless,
The strength is concrete,
The love surrounds their smiles.

I hurt inside,
The pain is real.
I'm told all of these wonderful things,
I'm told how lucky I am.

None of that changes reality,
None of that is an excuse to forget.
I can appreciate yet yearn,
I can love yet hate.

My family depends on me
I will always come through,
I am the rock my girls need me to be;
They are my heart.

Standing by their side,
Strong minded,
Strong passion,
I will love.

My wife is my reason.
She brightens my life,
Holds our family together,
Through every tough moment.

She is my ecstasy,
Her kiss brings me to my knees,
Her touch fills my heart,
Her love is unmatched.

Our daughters are our truth,
Our strength to overcome.
I will never let them know my pain,
They will only know monumental love.

I remain scared,
Hold fear close;
Fear will take me,
I will not let hate defeat me.

Why do we search for emptiness?
Learning to accept does not mean the end,
Rather a beginning of my acceptance.

MOTHER AND SON

From the time I understood
You were there,
You walked into my life without fear,
Your heart open and ready for me.

In a flash my life changed,
Young boy with no understanding,
Confused and hurt,
Tears of anger always present.

Quickly my heart had to love another,
No time to prepare.
She left without notice,
I was empty but not for long.

In a flash your life changed.
A woman who understood the challenge,
Ready to take care of me,
Ready to show me love.

You were as scared as I was,
You weren't allowed to show it.
Strong was all you knew,
Love was always given.

Years went by so quickly,
Birthday parties, games, school projects,
Passionate arguments,
Followed by equal apologies.

Unconditional love from a mother to her son,
Being a mother is so much more than being there on day 1.
Precious moments, happy or sad,
Followed by a lifetime of acceptance.

Challenges will always present themselves,
Unintentional hurtful moments arise,
Pain always finds its way into the heart,
When love is as strong as we are.

Those trying moments hang heavy on the heart,
When a simple apology doesn't have the needed impact,
That's when we must dig deep,
That's when we must love the most.

A bond between a mother and her son,
Is one only we understand;
These experiences are for us alone,
As we will always be there for each other.

SHARED HEART

Your eyes tell a story of strength,
You've seen love,
You've seen tragedy,
You've seen success.

Your heart makes you smile,
You've felt warmth,
You've felt pain,
You've pulled through.

Your mind amazes,
You've said, I do,
You've given life,
You provide.

I don't tell you enough, how much I love you.
I don't tell you enough, how amazing you are.
I don't tell you enough, how great you are to our family.
I don't tell you enough, how you've changed my life.

We are safe with you.
Our kids are growing up with your strength,
With your intelligence,
With your love.

I love how you make everything work,
I love how you're patient with us,
I love being your husband,
I love being your best friend.

We're in this together.
Nothing we can't accomplish.
We have so much more to conquer,
We have so much love to share.

SMOOTH WINE

One cold night,
Smooth, soft touch of your kiss,
Drawn to each other like a glass of wine to my lips,
I'd follow you anywhere as long as I'm with you.

Together we make it all work,
The kids, the house, they're everything to us.
We find solace in the woods,
Trail by trail our hearts are calm.

I cherish everyday with you,
I respect everything about you,
My love for you is a journey,
One that I want to be on for the rest of my life.

With moments of high intensity,
It's then that we have to be at our best.
Our love shows stronger,
Our kids watch with anticipation.

We must always be at our best,
When we feel like our worst,
Staying focused on our love
This is our time.

A FRIEND

Sincere thoughtfulness.
He listens when you achieve,
He listens when you fail,
He will always push you further.

His life stories are cherished,
Some have laughter,
Some have pain,
Some have strength.

We strive for acceptance from those we love,
When you don't have to look for it, it means the most.
It appears because you're worthy of that person's attention,
It evolves because you both care enough.

Some things in life don't have to be explained,
They just simply work.
Don't underestimate the importance of a friend,
They will always be there for you, no matter the challenge.

SECRETS

Memories are our secrets,
We keep them close,
Locked away in our minds,
The key is held by our hearts.

Strength born from love,
Increments of tiny specs of dirt,
Forcing their way into our home,
Each step brings us closer.

PAIN

People are hurting,
They feel trapped in this open world,
Scared from within,
Frightened souls need help.

Don't ignore the pain,
Shed tears through truth;
Feeling sad is real,
Help me by hearing me.

BLIND RAGE

Frightened cries in her sleep,
Force terror into the mind;
Blind rage is upon him,
There's no way out.

Darkness fills the body,
Clawing at his insides,
Burning every thought
Into dust.

Please make it stop.
Why must this continue?
Every way out is a brick wall,
Leading to a bloody mess.

Crouching in the corner,
Red towels spread across the floor,
Screaming has calmed,
Pain has now surfaced.

Control is out of reach,
Don't know what to do,
Needing this to stop,
Help this man.

EMPTY TRUTH

Honesty is the scariest emotion.
How do I feel when I am scorned?
How can I pick myself up after being beaten so badly?
When will this truth come out?

Spending countless dark nights waiting,
Always waiting, never moving along;
I want you all to know,
I can never show you.

She was there so innocently,
Her mind was muddy,
Never meaning to hurt,
That's when she hurt the most.

When will I cease to blame myself
To blame her?
It may not be her fault,
That road was paved from the start.

Going back fifty years,
Digging deep within the crust,
Searching for fire,
Never finding smoke.

The truth does exist;
The truth will always haunt.
Stop asking for it;
Why do I need it?

Love should be enough;
Trust should be enough.
It never will be;
The mystery will go on…

FEAR

His memories are clear,
Fear is the unknown.
Made up stories,
Clear path to destruction.

Not allowed to be angry,
Not allowed to remember.
Move on, grow up,
Don't think so much.

The fear seems to be from the provider,
Strength is not shown through fear.
Being feared means being respected;
He fears for this path.

His actions make a difference,
He impacts those around him.
Weakness shown daily;
Blind to this reality.

MY SMILE

Finding yourself never stops.
Pressure to be successful.
We want everything,
Looking in the wrong direction.

Years of searching,
I may have found myself.
What makes me proud and happy?
Stop yearning for something I can't see.

Three women have changed my
life. I work smarter, I live
stronger, My smile is finally
real,
Genuine happiness in front of me.

GOOD IS EASY

I don't want to argue,
I'm a happy man,
I want to smile,
I want to love.

I can never ease my way through;
Struggles are real.
The ability to overcome without further pain,
That's my challenge.

Take a step back,
Don't get caught up,
The wrong vision can distort the goal,
Win or lose the fight, always lose the battle.

I will focus on love,
I will continue to work.
Good is easy,
Bad takes effort.

COLORFUL VOICE

Colorful begins the tale,
Shouting out to a Stranger,
Allowing the unknown into my life,
Without hesitation.

I hold my moments close,
Days, Weeks, Months,
We allow them to pass,
We allow them to grow.

Always knowing we come back,
Always sharing our paths,
Views at Walden Pond,
Singing at Red Lights.

A voice that speaks to my heart,
Sends a vibe through my body,
Spreading Love through vision,
A love that stays with me.

You are everyone's friend,
You are everyone's happy face.
You bring smiles to moments that need them most,
You are always there even when I can't see you.

For every smile you create,
This is the time to give back.
Gathering every happy moment,
Holding in our hearts your amazement.

PROUD

This is where he starts,
Putting his jacket on alone,
Walking his mind to school,
He must get out of the madness.

He took a risk on a woman,
Finding heartbreak in his path.
The pain was masked,
The pain was real.

Two innocent minds,
Became his only reason.
They would be protected,
Shielded from the destruction.

His way of life was at risk,
His father was there to help,
He fought his way through,
Never looking back.

100 miles an hour with blinders on,
No one would alter his path.
He would succeed at his way,
Failing had no place.

We may not always understand,
We may challenge his ideas,
We may struggle with the reasons,
We will question everything.

But we love who he has become,
Understand who he is,
Proud he's on our side,
Lucky to share this life with him.

He shares his moments with his best friend,
She provides strength for him,
She will test his mind,
He welcomes this life.

His granddaughters breathe new life,
Holding close to his heart.
They are the reason he smiles,
The truth behind his happiness.

He may mask what I share here,
He may never speak a word,
But we know who this man is,
We're proud he's on our side.

He started his walk alone,
Never looking back.
Now we share this road with him,
We are lucky to have him.

LOVE AND RESPECT

A man who has lost so much,
Something that was taken from him,
Cheated out of an experience,
A love stolen from his heart.

Yet what remains is tremendous love,
A family that is real,
Moments that are created out of purity;
He still has much to create.

His wife by his side, sharing their loss,
She's the force that encourages strength,
His best friend with every step,
Traveling around the world as one.

His smile is seen through his girls,
They look up to him,
They need him,
They admire him.

Stopping to smell the fresh air is wasting time,
He needs to keep moving,
He needs constant direction,
Nothing left to chance.

His family admires his ways,
Although the energy does not live in them the same way,
Taking a step back,
Sitting with calmness.

Admiring the beauty of the mountains,
Staring out into the ocean.
This time is what they need,
The path isn't always paved.

Together they see common ground,
Patience with each other,
Love and respect,
This man has it all.

WRITER

From the start my path was set,
Innocence filled my youth.
Too young to share my voice,
Too scared to share my fear.

Asking questions of why,
Only answered with "that's what we do".
Simplicity created my fight,
Never enough to go around.

Filled with confusion,
Anger stayed with me,
Never knowing the way out,
Follow the path that is laid out for me.

Jealous minds surround my existence.
I owe those who can't,
I owe those who want,
I simply just owe.

The years that start to matter,
Still are unanswered.
Too scared to share my fear,
This path is uneasy.

Is this what I want to do?
When do I ask that question?
When am I allowed to answer honestly?
When will my fear leave me?

Finding out who we are,
Common mistakes,
Surround this man,
Falling as fast as I stand.

As I write,
I ask again,
What do I want to do?
What can I be?

We don't become what we do,
We are who we are all along.
The courage to speak,
Finds truth.

I am a writer;
I find nothing simple in that.
I am filled with genuine happiness,
While I do this.

Conquer my enemies,
I am ready to share my fear,
Wanderer at best,
As I write.

PROTECTED HEART

Innocent mind of a toddler,
Her bright blue eyes have only wonder,
Questions she doesn't know to ask yet,
Reasons to be scared don't show.

Protected by her shadow.
Learn to eat,
Learn to dress,
Learn to smile.

Her heart is secure.
Within her mind she holds so close,
A woman of great strength,
Persistent to hide the truths.

Faced with the greatest challenge of her life,
Smiling through it all.
Laughter fills the hospital bed,
Fear has no place here.

Always surpassing the obstacles,
She delivers with force.
Proud of who she's become,
Who she has yet to be.

Wife,
Mother,
Daughter,
Sister.

She breaks all barriers,
Continues to succeed with each level.

Mindful of her needs,
Careful with her heart.

Protected at every moment.
We are one at our core,
Even when we scare each other,
We can bend but never break.

DEVIL'S VALUE

We all look for peace,
Some open their eyes with it,
Making their path an easy one;
Calmness fills their world.

Some learn about it,
Move dirt and rocks to uncover,
Appearing to dig through the heat;
A ghost of innocence.

He appears from the ashes,
Moving his way through the dust.
He will have his way,
When the time is right.

Confidence with every spoken word,
Fear ghosted behind the walls,
Laughter in the devil's eye,
He will find his way.

His drive is unknown,
Scary to the observer.
These bullets can't stop him—
The gun was never loaded.

They thought they took everything from him.
But you can't take from someone,
If you don't know what they value;
They trusted phantom dreams.

Truth is what they desire—
Often met with great resistance.
Offering peace with a bloody knife,
Maybe he'll give it to them.

ESCAPE

Driving down a dirt road,
Hands hanging out the window,
No direction set,
This road leads everywhere.

Leave it all behind:
The faults,
The achievements,
Leave them.

Ahead is purity.
Questions don't arise,
Fear has no place,
Released from the Devil.

Into the arms of no one.
That feeling at the end,
They say you can't achieve,
Impossible to breathe that moment.

Their faults weight heavy on your goals,
Their fears keep you from overcoming yours.
Held down by the past,
Awaiting release.

No matter how fast you run,
How hard you push,
You can't escape their fears.
You own them now.

WORRY-FREE WORLD

Worry-free world,
I don't live in it.
I hear the thoughts of lost souls,
Violently running through the crowd.

It's here that I seek my value,
Never seeming to find what makes me smile.
A glimmer of hope,
Always shut down.

An overwhelming happiness
Takes over.
She passes through me,
So quickly, I don't see her soul.

That truly is what I need.
Without this love,
Emptiness fills this world;
Alone is what we'll be.

Needing to wake up and feel her,
Watch her sleep with her tenderness.
Her cheeks sparkle like a million grains of sand,
Lying still under the stars.

Worry-free world,
I don't think it exists.
The thoughts bring me to my knees,
This powerful love is upon me.

DESIRE

At times we feel a loss,
Common to our hearts,
Falling to the ground,
As a drifting snowflake.

Searching for the true moment,
Feeling emptiness,
Accompanied by truth,
Distraught by nature.

This is the love that I have,
Creations abruptly stopped;
Failure throughout the colony,
Pressure arrives by loss.

We hold this moment,
Impatiently lusting over our desire,
Arriving in unknown forces,
She has appeared.

Shadowing the fears,
Standing tall,
Never forgetting why she's there,
Never losing her passion.

Creating this space,
We occupy with strength;
Awaiting beauty,
With desire to love.

WANDERER

Young boy peeking over the edge,
Nothing but waves in his way,
Pretending to be surrounded,
By the naked truth.

He's alone with these secrets,
Capturing more will only haunt the dust;
How much risk can he take,
Without the fear of loss?

Years of riding down black holes,
There is the only place of reason;
Generations of simply existing,
Only wandering the path that is given.

A different path is taken,
That will frighten the weak behind him;
An old dirt road will uncover,
Calm truth.

Shots fired.

HER TRUTH

Driving around empty streets
Never knowing if she'll see you again
Tolerant in your deception
Your dreams are left behind

Everyone she knew had a purpose
Everyone she knows lost the hand
Twisted emotions falling fast
Darkness will have its way

Forced into a dark hole
She never could never be allowed to speak
Her intentions remained dormant
Screaming from inside

They will have their way
The more she fights the path
The more her loss will show
Pretending swallows her pain

Her peace sits in the distance
Too far to see
Her need to find her truth
Continues her fight

GHOST SHEPHERD

He is a good person
Standing alone at the bottom
Heat rising all around
Death looms upon a bloody pole

The smell of defeat
Rising through this pain
Wandering through the desert
Searching for diamonds

He finds nothing but sharp edges
Clawing away at his heart
Excruciating existence looms
Why has this happened to him?

Realizing the truth has never been more scary
He is here to protect
His death means life for many others
His blood will be drank forever

The significance relies heavily on who has bestowed his crown
No soul has accepted a greater power
Ones who don't deserve the chance
Love that needs explanation

He will be by your side
Deep inside your dark heart
From the tips of your beauty
Never leaving you

His death is your life
Handle this gift with pride
Don't force this darkness
For he will awaken the demons

Remember him when you smile
When you make someone sad
Your first unimaginable love
Your first defeat

He is with you.

I IMAGINE

I imagine you don't know me well
Pretending to be a friend
Waking closely by my side
Your efforts are lost quickly

These days are where it starts
Needing double what it takes
Searching for truth
Never peeling back the failure

You can't comprehend this level
Reaching out with one fragile hand
Your heart bleeds this pain
Wanting so bad to be felt

I imagine this is where I leave you
Struggling to see the ghost
Open our eyes
Don't let him leave

Simple actions of friendship
Where are you?
I see bright lights coming at me
Jumping on this train seems the only way

Out of town
Down the dirt road
Pebbles and muddy steps
This is where I'll find you

YOSHI

Who will protect me now?
The innocence surrounding our lives.
You helped me grow,
always by my side.

I found you alone in the driveway,
helped you realize my love was real
I made you part of my life;
the connection was instant.

We traveled a long distance,
my sanity pushed to the edge,
never knowing if we'd make it,
uncertain if I ever could.

We promptly found the reason,
every step together, getting closer to why
Loving every moment with you
we took this trip as one

I hold your heart with me
As I resume this journey
Traveling together,
Taxi rides will never be the same

I'm grateful for our path
Your playfulness taught me strength;
Your sweetness made me smile.
I will miss everything about you

Thank you for our time together.

REMAIN SILENT

A dark room with a pure scent;
Lonely bottle sitting by the fireplace.
Gently poured onto the ice;
The crackling fills the room.

This is the time to listen;
Let the taste consume you.
Sit back in that deep leather chair,
Forget why you're there.

Distinct smell is upon you;
You need this moment.
What makes you cry,
Has been forgotten.

What makes you happy,
Is a memory.
You hold emptiness tightly;
And fill the glass once more.

This is the time to learn;
Silence is your companion.
The dirt in the road passes through your mind,
Dust devouring your soul.

The mountains seep into your glass,
Each sip brings you closer to the delusion;
That you are alone.
You have much to learn.

The darkness if warned,
Will harvest this moment.
Trust the silence,
It will bring you peace.

THE ONE

Crisp evening, moon shinning bright;
That look in your eye, could tonight be the night?
Just dinner with a girl, you're just not sure.
Gone in a moment when I opened the door.

I laughed at your jokes, smiles poured through;
Sweet potato rolls, my mind is on you.
This Brookline night excitement in the air;
A sweet kiss, I was almost in the clear.

Top of the mountain we go, you said yes.
Then the fun starts, inviting the guests.
A beautiful night surrounded by love.
A beautiful start staring down from above.

Off to Needham we go, our little ones are ready.
Home, picket fence, our hands our steady.
We patiently waited, with much suspense;
They came into this world, from the start, intense.

Sparkle in her eye, sweet sounds at night.
Everything we wanted, leave on the light.
You're the mother of angles, beautiful and strong.
You deserve every moment that comes along.

You are the love of my life, proud and true;
I am lucky to spend the rest of my life with you.

DELIVERANCE

What does the patient mind tell you?
Can you see through the wall?
Seek the only common ground;
Becoming dirty from the inside.

Hidden beneath this depth
Lies significant truth.
Crusty in its appearance,
Clear upon delivery.

What scares you about silence?
Why does the idea bring you to your knees?
Beauty waits while you quiver;
Overcome your fear to see this peace.

Your kindred awaited your truth,
Don't let that slip away.
Your distracted eyes seek injustice;
The path you're on has become bumpy.

What you need, is deliverance.
A soul to keep you upright.
Gutlessness of the keeper,
Will become your savior.

We find distraction with deceit.
The hunter changes roles;
Now looking over the shoulder.
Outrun the hunt or lay beneath the dirt.

The calmness sets in.
There is beauty beyond what you see.
You will have what you need.
These moments won't define you.

Seek the justice within.
You will always remain.
The pain is hidden with control.
You will need strength to keep it there.

What surrounds you, is all you need.
The grins of youth become tranquility.
Stability is your force,
Become what you set out to be.

ALONE

Hidden from the light.
Abandoned with his thoughts.
Salt drips down his face,
Escaping the existence.

Eyes look to the mountain,
Colors reflecting.
Snow caps in the distance,
Calmness sets in.

The Giant has awoken,
His deception grows wild.
Finding his truth down the dirt road.
This unlikely soul becomes his gem.

Fault hidden beneath the canopy,
Judgement guides his weakness.
Scared and cold,
Absent in his own artistry.

This is the only safe place.
His secret to climb into this hole.
The one moment control is his.
Staying here is the only way.

Feeling detached,
Needing significance.
Finding emptiness,
Completely alone.

LEARNED BEHAVIOR

We aren't born to hate,
We rise with a smile.
Caring for one another,
Compassionate with our first word.

It's you who has left this mark.
While you sit back,
Destruction lays below.
Is this what you wanted?

Where did this seed begin?
Was the water jug empty?
Why are you so harmful?
Why is this road so severe?

This empathy is getting old.
Complications from sun up,
Annihilation at sun down.
Desolate promises.

I'm frustrated by your perception.
It's frightening to learn from your pain.
What your eyes have seen,
Should steer your teachings.

Still, you stay the course.
It now becomes my determination,
Not to implode.
To flush the creator out of the woods.

The absurdity of this land,
Spills out of the glass.
It's dark warm color,
Fills my body.

I am here to be the change,
Untie my hands.
I want peace for you,
For your land.

Looking out to the fire burning your forest.
Do you search for the nearest water?
Or do you enjoy the inferno?
This catastrophic nature is beneath you.

I accept this burden for change.
You must wonder why I'm so different.
Why I seek answers,
My reflection is not enraged.

I am tolerant with your demise,
Ardent on this path.
Truth will transform this trail.
The hunter mentality won't last long.

THE REASON

The Truth is, I don't have a clue.
Don't know where I'm headed,
Can't say where I've been.
Dumbfounded by the discovery.

I write these poems as thoughts on a napkin.
I never seem to use it to clean up.
The mess is apparent,
Emptiness won't surprise you.

I go back to the beginning,
Looking for a reason.
The soft sand under my feet,
Warmth of the ocean overcomes me.

I spend nights underneath the trees,
When I speak, they respond.
What a feeling it is to have nature talk back.
Some of the best conversations are withheld.

Now the freshness of corduroy is beneath my feet,
Crisp air in my face.
Sun glaring down on me.
Leave me here, I'm peaceful.